Original title:
Icy Tufts Along the Faerie Drip

Author: Linda Leevike
ISBN HARDBACK: 978-1-80559-394-2
ISBN PAPERBACK: 978-1-80559-893-0

Celestial Frost and Whispering Leaves

In twilight's grasp, a silence falls,
Where frosty whispers ride the breeze.
The leaves, they dance, in soft refrains,
Beneath a sky that softly gleams.

A silver veil on earth is laid,
As shadows stretch and softly play.
Each crystal droplet, pure and bright,
Reflects the night in gentle sway.

Stars twinkle high, with frosted grace,
Illuminating nature's quilt.
In whispers soft, the night unfolds,
As dreams and wishes gently tilt.

The moon adorns the tranquil night,
With beams that touch the quiet ground.
The world wrapped tight in winter's wrap,
In magic's hold, we're tightly bound.

In this embrace of frost and light,
We find the peace the heart requires.
Celestial wonders, all around,
Awake our warmth, ignite the fires.

Frosted Visions Dancing in the Mist

A shroud of mist, a breath of freeze,
Curling around the slumbering trees.
In every breath, a vision glows,
Frosted dreams where silence flows.

Nature's canvas, brushed with white,
Each twig adorned in sparkling light.
The air is crisp, the world still sleeps,
As frozen magic softly creeps.

Whispers of frost in the early dawn,
As shadows fade and night is gone.
A shimmer hugs the earth below,
In frosted visions, joy will grow.

Among the pines, the secrets hide,
In every flake where dreams abide.
Dancing softly in wintry grace,
The mist unveils a secret place.

With every step, the echoes call,
In frosted visions, we find it all.
Our hearts entwined in nature's weave,
In every glimmer, we believe.

Secrets of the Glimmering Glade

In glades where sunlight softly plays,
With shadows cast in gentle haze,
The secrets of the earth conceal,
In whispers low, the heart can feel.

A glimmer shines through emerald leaves,
Where nature's breath in silence weaves.
Each rustling sound, a story told,
In glimmering paths of green and gold.

Crickets sing in twilight's hue,
As stars awake in skies of blue.
The gentle breeze, a lover's sigh,
In glades of secrets, we pass by.

Among the ferns, a world appears,
With every rustle, allures our fears.
In tranquil hearts, the mysteries lay,
Revealing truths in soft array.

Beneath the moon's caress, we roam,
In glimmering glades, we find our home.
A tapestry of night unfolds,
In secrets whispered, love beholds.

Dreamy Frost on a Celestial Breeze

A gentle touch of icy breath,
Cascades of white weave tales of death.
In dreams we wander, lost in time,
With frosty kisses, hearts entwined.

Celestial winds, they softly sigh,
As sparkling layers drift and lie.
Each flake a wish, a hope, a dream,
In slumber's hold, we float downstream.

The night unfolds its silken veil,
As frost ignites the moonlit trail.
In dreamy whispers, we take flight,
On paths adorned with purest light.

As shadows blend and night descends,
The world is hushed, as time suspends.
In frosted realms where silence flows,
The heart remembers what love knows.

With every breath, a tale to weave,
Under the stars, we dare believe.
In the dreams of frost, a solace found,
On celestial breezes, love unbound.

Frosted Whispers in Enchanted Glades

In glades where shadows softly lie,
A frosted hush, a gentle sigh.
Whispers dance on winter's breath,
Secrets shared in icy depth.

Stars twinkle through the branches bare,
Casting dreams upon the air.
Nature's lullaby, sweet and clear,
A symphony for those who hear.

Beneath the boughs, the world awaits,
Mysteries spun through frosty gates.
Each flake a tale of time and space,
Nature's art in pure embrace.

Echoes linger, soft and bright,
Glowing softly in the night.
Frosted trails of silver hue,
Lead the wanderer to the dew.

With every step, the ground will yield,
A hidden path through nature's shield.
Where whispers weave through ancient trees,
And the heart finds its gentle ease.

Crystals Whisper Secrets of the Night

Crystals gleam in moonlit pools,
Whispering secrets, ancient rules.
Night unfolds its velvet shroud,
Nature sings, both soft and loud.

Fragrant winds bring tales anew,
Carried softly, crisp and true.
Shadows dance on pathways bright,
Dreams unfurl in starlit flight.

Beneath the dome of skies so wide,
Lurks a magic none can hide.
Crystals gather, voices blend,
In the stillness, messages send.

Each shimmering light, a story spun,
Tales of joy, of battles won.
In the hush, a call to see,
Whispers woven into harmony.

Awake in wonder, hearts ignite,
Crystals whisper secrets of the night.
In stillness, mysteries ignite a spark,
Guiding dreams through the dark.

Glistening Veils Under Moonlit Boughs

Underneath the moon's soft rays,
Glistening veils steal breath away.
Silvery threads of night entwine,
In the silence, stars align.

Boughs adorned with twinkling lace,
Nature's charm in a sacred space.
Every rustle tells a tale,
Of wandering hearts that never fail.

Veils of mist, a gentle shroud,
Whispers echo, low and loud.
Glistening paths beneath the sway,
Lead the lost and the astray.

The night reveals her hidden charms,
Cradled softly in nature's arms.
Every moment, a chance to breathe,
In the beauty that we weave.

Underneath the vast expanse,
Glistening veils invite a dance.
In moonlight's glow, we find our place,
Connected to the night's embrace.

Ethereal Frost and Shimmering Delights

Ethereal frost on window panes,
Captures whispers of our refrains.
Shimmering delights, a fleeting sight,
Glimmer softly in morning light.

Nature's lace upon the ground,
In delicate patterns, peace is found.
With every breath, a story told,
In the shimmer, life unfolds.

A canvas painted, pure and bright,
Ethereal whispers take to flight.
Frosty kisses on tender leaves,
In every corner, magic weaves.

Glistening echoes of frosty light,
Chase the shadows of the night.
Delights awaken, senses keen,
In the quiet, tranquil scene.

Among the frost, our spirits soar,
Ethereal frost opens the door.
To wonders hidden from the sight,
In nature's heart, we find delight.

Resplendent Frost on Faerie Wings

In twilight's grasp, the faeries play,
With shimmering wings, they dance and sway.
Each icy breath a spark of light,
Transforming dreams from dark to bright.

Glistening trails on gentle breeze,
They whisper secrets through the trees.
A tapestry of silver spun,
Wrapped in the warmth of winter's sun.

In crystal gardens, magic blooms,
Frost-kissed petals chase away glooms.
A glimmering world wrapped in grace,
Where time stands still in this wondrous place.

With laughter ringing, sweet and clear,
They beckon forth the night, so dear.
In their embrace, the stars align,
In resplendent frost, their hearts entwine.

In slumber's gaze, the world reflects,
The mystic dance the night connects.
With every breath, a tale they weave,
On faerie wings, we dare to believe.

Ephemeral Frost in the Heart of Enchantment

Ephemeral frost upon the ground,
Lays a blanket soft, without a sound.
Each crystal flake a fleeting sigh,
A moment's beauty, time slips by.

In enchanted woods, the whispers flow,
Magic lingers in the soft, pale glow.
The moonlight gently paints the scene,
A fleeting dream in silver sheen.

Between the branches, shadows play,
As frost embraces the twilight's sway.
Each breath of wind holds tales untold,
Of fleeting magic, brave and bold.

In the heart of night, spirits roam,
Entwined with frost, they find their home.
Each glimmering pause, a chance to see,
The beauty wrapped in epiphany.

As dawn approaches, the frost will fade,
But in our hearts, the echoes stayed.
For in the magic that we chase,
We find a warmth, a sweet embrace.

Frosted Lullabies Beneath the Glimmering Stars

Underneath the stars, so bright,
Whispers float upon the night.
Frosted lullabies softly hum,
Guiding dreams as shadows come.

Each note a shimmer, cool and light,
Wraps the world in pure delight.
In slumber's hold, the heart takes flight,
Where frost and dreams unite so tight.

The nightingale sings in frozen trees,
Carried forth on a gentle breeze.
A symphony of night unfolds,
In glistening hush, pure magic holds.

As frost blankets the sleeping land,
Nights of wonder close at hand.
Each twinkle reflects hopes anew,
In lullabies the stars imbue.

When dawn peeks in with golden rays,
The frosted dreams softly embrace.
Yet in our hearts, the echoes stay,
Of frosted lullabies and starry play.

Snowbound Sentinels of the Mystic Realm

Guardians stand in snow's embrace,
Sentinels of this sacred place.
With silent strength, they watch and wait,
In the stillness, they contemplate.

Their breath creates a misty veil,
On winter's path, where whispers sail.
In armored white, so still, so grand,
They cradle secrets of this land.

Each flake a story, ancient, wise,
As snowflakes dance from hidden skies.
They weave the fables of the night,
In shimmering gowns of purest white.

Through frosted pines and silver streams,
The sentinels guard our deepest dreams.
In every flurry, every chill,
A promise echoes, soft and still.

As twilight fades and shadows crawl,
Their presence lingers, through it all.
For in the snowbound, heart's own realm,
The mystic depth is at the helm.

Frosty Hues on the Canvas of Sleep

In the hush of night's embrace,
Whispers dance on silver lace.
Dreams wrapped in a chilly grace,
Frosty hues, a softened space.

Blankets thick with quiet frost,
Memories gleam, never lost.
Stars like gems in dark embossed,
Night becomes a soothing coast.

Swaying branches, branches bare,
Crystals hanging in the air.
Gentle echoes of a prayer,
On this canvas, dreams declare.

Each breath flows like whispering lace,
Mapping journeys, time and place.
Through the night, we find our grace,
In frosty hues, our hearts embrace.

Morning light will break the spell,
Warming tales that we can tell.
In the frost, our secrets dwell,
Painting sleep with magic's swell.

A Zephyr's Kiss in Winter's Court

A zephyr's kiss upon the cheek,
Soft and tender, calm and meek.
In winter's court, the days are sleek,
With frozen whispers, nature speaks.

Snowflakes twirl, a ballet grand,
Blanketing the slumbering land.
Each crystal formed by nature's hand,
A fleeting moment, soft and planned.

Branches bow with laden grace,
While shadows dance in gentle space.
Winter's beauty leaves no trace,
Yet warms the heart in its embrace.

Evenings glow with amber light,
As stars emerge to greet the night.
Underneath the moon's soft sight,
Dreams take flight in sheer delight.

A zephyr's kiss, a fleeting thrill,
Filling hearts with winter's chill.
In each breath, we hear the still,
Of winter's song, a magic quill.

Crystal Visions in the Frosty Glade

In the glade where silence weaves,
Crystal visions, the heart believes.
Every breath the winter leaves,
A spark of life the cold retrieves.

Trees adorned in glistening white,
Captured dreams in the soft twilight.
Magic spills in soft twilight,
Bright reflections, pure delight.

Echoes whisper of the past,
Frozen moments that will last.
In the stillness, shadows cast,
A gentle sigh, the die is cast.

With every step, the world a glow,
Footprints trace where no one goes.
In the silence, beauty grows,
As crystal visions start to show.

Frosty air sweetens the night,
Each breath a chance, a pure invite.
In the glade, our spirits light,
Dancing softly in the white.

The Enigma of Winter's Faerie Light

In the woods where shadows play,
Winter's faerie lights display.
Softly glowing, drift away,
Enigmas dance in dusk's ballet.

Glistening trails of misty dew,
A shimmering path where dreams break through.
Cloaked in silence, the night anew,
Winter's magic in each view.

Whispers of the ancient trees,
Breathe the secrets in the breeze.
In this realm, where time appease,
We find a joy that never flees.

Faerie lights, an otherworldly sight,
Guide our souls with soft delight.
In frozen realms, we take to flight,
Following dreams in the moonlight.

The enigma calls us to explore,
Where winter's heart begins to soar.
In every glimmer, we implore,
To chase the magic forevermore.

Frosty Clusters of Whispers Untold

In the twilight's gentle glow,
Frosty whispers dance and flow,
Clustered dreams on the winter's breath,
Secrets frozen, weaving death.

Softly falling, flakes of white,
Wrap the world in purest light,
Stories hidden beneath the sheen,
In the silence, all is seen.

Breezes carry silent songs,
Through the trees where frost belongs,
Each breath a chill, each sigh a plea,
Nature's pulse, a tapestry.

Footprints linger on the ground,
Echoes of the lost, profound,
Lost in time, the night unfolds,
Frosty clusters, whispers bold.

Beneath the stars, the air is crisp,
Nature's art, a frosted lisp,
In these clusters, life entwined,
Untold stories, undefined.

Elegance of Winter in the Faerie's Breath

In the hush of twilight's embrace,
Faerie whispers leave no trace,
A dance of snowflakes, soft and light,
Painting elegance in the night.

Glistening trees, adorned in white,
Held in rapture, pure delight,
Where the moonbeams softly play,
In winter's arms, dreams stray away.

Sequins of frost on the meadow's cloak,
Every shimmer, a loving stroke,
Faerie's breath, a tender sigh,
Carrying wishes to the sky.

Crystals formed from fleeting dew,
In the silence, all is new,
Charmed by whispers, night unfolds,
Stories spun in silver and gold.

In the elegance of this scene,
Winter's magic felt, unseen,
A breath of faeries, soft and sweet,
Where the human and magical meet.

Enchanted Frost on Faerie Paths

Upon the paths where faeries tread,
Enchanted frost, a silken thread,
Sparkling trails in the pale moonlight,
Whispers linger, soft and light.

Gentle sighs of the winter breeze,
Carrying tales through the frozen trees,
Each step awakens the sleeping ground,
Frosty secrets, in silence, abound.

A tapestry of white unfurled,
Cascading beauty, a hidden world,
In every flake, a story spins,
Of faerie courts where magic begins.

Tiny footprints leave their mark,
In the stillness, bright and stark,
Kiss of frost on the evening air,
Every moment, enchantments flare.

Underneath the starry dome,
Whispers guide the faeries home,
Through enchanted frost, they glide,
In the magic where dreams abide.

The Frozen Rhapsody of a Moonlit Tale

Beneath the moon's ethereal glow,
A frozen rhapsody begins to flow,
Tales of winter, soft and bright,
Unraveled treasures of the night.

In the silence, stories weave,
Each snowflake a dream to believe,
Whispers carried on the wind,
In this rhapsody, we ascend.

Trees adorned in crystal grace,
Holding magic in their embrace,
As shadows dance, the night alights,
With every breath, the heart ignites.

Echoes of laughter fill the space,
In a world where time leaves no trace,
Moonlit paths call us near,
To the tales only we can hear.

Embrace the chill, let spirits rise,
Under a cosmos of starry skies,
The frozen rhapsody we hold near,
In winter's clutch, love draws us here.

Frosted Whispers Under Starlit Canopies

In the hush of night,
Whispers softly dance,
Beneath the starlit sky,
Nature's sweet romance.

Frosted leaves glisten,
Moonlight's gentle touch,
Secrets held in silence,
Nature knows so much.

Shadows play and sway,
In the peeling night,
Echoes of the past,
Glow with pure delight.

Branches bow and sway,
Under silver beams,
Tender dreams awaken,
Cradled in moonbeams.

Songs of winter winds,
Chanting through the trees,
Frosted whispers call,
Through the twilight breeze.

Glimmers of Enchantment in the Winter Grove

Amidst the snowflakes,
Glimmers softly shine,
Every breath of cold,
Magic intertwine.

Frosty patterns weave,
On branches bare and bright,
In the winter grove,
Shimmers in the night.

Hidden treasures twink,
Underneath the frost,
Every gentle step,
A moment not lost.

Nature's quiet spell,
Cast in hues of white,
Glimmers of enchantment,
Fill the silent night.

Through the sparkling trees,
A dance in the air,
Winter's sweet embrace,
Whispers everywhere.

Shimmering Veils on the Edge of Dreams

In the night's embrace,
Veils of silver swirl,
Carrying the dreams,
Of every boy and girl.

Shimmers in the dark,
Dancing on the stream,
Floating on the wind,
Carrying a dream.

Whispers in the night,
Secrets softly hum,
On the edge of sleep,
A world yet to come.

Stars above us twirl,
In a whimsical waltz,
Painting ghostly trails,
As the night exalts.

Through shimmering veils,
Our wishes take flight,
Luring us to chase,
The magic of night.

Sparkling Ferns Beneath the Moonlit Stream

By the moonlit stream,
Ferns begin to spark,
Cascading lights twinkle,
Lighting up the dark.

Softly rustling leaves,
Whispering their tale,
Under silver rays,
Rivers start to sail.

Waves of twinkling light,
Glistening like dreams,
Dancing in the flow,
Of moonlit gentle beams.

Secret worlds awake,
Where the waters gleam,
Sparkling ferns unite,
Under nature's theme.

In this tranquil space,
Magic softly beams,
As we wander on,
Through everlasting dreams.

Glistening Trinkets on the Frostbitten Path

Amidst the snowflakes dancing bright,
Glistening treasures catch the light.
Each one a whisper of tales untold,
On a path where stories unfold.

Footprints trace a journey near,
Wrapped in a blanket of winter's cheer.
Nature's jewels in silence gleam,
Painting a landscape of frozen dreams.

Every step a soft embrace,
In this icy, enchanted space.
Caught in a moment, time stands still,
Heartbeats echo with winter's thrill.

With every glance, magic's spark,
Illuminates the chill and dark.
The path ahead, a shimmering tide,
Where memories and secrets abide.

In the frosty air where shadows play,
Glistening trinkets light the way.
Gathered dreams in every flake,
Glimmers of joy we create and make.

The Frozen Caress of Whimsical Dreams

In the stillness, dreams arise,
Wrapped in whispers, winter skies.
A frozen breath on soft, pale skin,
Where wonder waits to draw you in.

Whimsical visions drift and dance,
Like snowflakes caught in playful trance.
Each gentle touch, a fleeting thought,
In the magic of dreams, we are caught.

Silvery echoes of laughter ring,
Within the chill, our hearts take wing.
In this realm of frost and grace,
We find our solace, our sacred space.

Transported to where wishes flow,
Beneath the twilight's gentle glow.
Each moment woven, rich and rare,
In the frozen caress, love is bare.

With every heartbeat, the night unfolds,
Softly weaving tales like threads of gold.
Embraced by frost, we spin and dream,
In enchanted radiance, we gleam.

Chilling Lullabies of Enchantment's Glow

Underneath the starry night,
Chilling lullabies take flight.
Echoes of a gentle tune,
In the silver light of the moon.

Softly sung by winter's breath,
Stories of life entwined with death.
Through the air, a soothing song,
In the stillness, we belong.

Frosted whispers kiss the trees,
Carried softly by the breeze.
Enchantment wraps the world in peace,
As worries fade and troubles cease.

With each note, a memory stirs,
A dance of snowflakes, winter purrs.
Nature's cadence, a tender embrace,
In chilling lullabies we find grace.

As dreams entwine in frosty air,
We breathe in magic, hearts laid bare.
In the hush of night we stay,
Guided by the enchantment's sway.

Luminous Fables on the Frosted Air

Fables spin in winter's breath,
Luminous tales of life and death.
Each shimmering word, a glint of light,
Dancing softly in the night.

On frosted air, stories glide,
Each whisper carries dreams inside.
In every sparkle, hope ignites,
As magic fills the starry nights.

Listen close to the tales that weave,
In every flake, what we believe.
Stories of love, of joy, despair,
Floating gently in the chilly air.

Glowing paths where heartstrings play,
Fables guiding us on our way.
In the twilight, eyes will shine,
With luminous wonders, divine.

As frost embraces every sound,
In the silence, warmth is found.
Fables told beneath the stars,
Remind us who we really are.

Glacial Dreams in the Glade of Dreams

In the glade where shadows play,
Glacial whispers in the fray.
Starry night, a velvet sky,
Dreams entwine as time slips by.

Crystals dance on icy streams,
Painting visions, woven dreams.
Winds of winter softly call,
In this realm, we rise and fall.

Evergreen, a silent watch,
Moonlit glades, a gentle touch.
Memory drifts like frosted air,
In this moment, free from care.

Echoes of the past still roam,
Within the glacial, sacred home.
As dawn breaks with a golden hue,
We awaken, born anew.

Bejeweled Dewdrops on Luminous Leaves

Morning light in silver beams,
Dewdrops gleam with whispered dreams.
Nature's jewels on emerald lace,
Sparkling in the sun's warm grace.

Every drop a tale to tell,
Caught in magic, cast a spell.
Whispers ride the gentle breeze,
Rustling softly through the trees.

Petals glisten, colors bright,
A dance of joy, sheer delight.
In this garden, life abounds,
Harmony in nature's sounds.

As the day begins to fade,
Rays of gold in twilight wade.
Dewdrops catch the last light's kiss,
In this moment, purest bliss.

The Frost's Embrace on the Faerie Paths

Along the paths where fairies tread,
Frosty whispers, lightly spread.
Luminous trails in moonlight bright,
Glimmers dance in the hush of night.

Silver tendrils weave and twine,
In the air, a magic sign.
Each step taken, soft and light,
Frost's embrace in gentle flight.

Crystals glint in hidden nooks,
Secrets held in ancient books.
Where the earth and magic blend,
Time stands still, no need to mend.

As dawn approaches, shadows fade,
In the frost, our dreams are laid.
Faerie paths will call us near,
With every breath, their song we hear.

Glimpse of Magic in a Wintry Lattice

In the stillness, magic stirs,
Through the lattice, winter purrs.
Fractal patterns, delicate lace,
Each flake falls, a soft embrace.

Hidden whispers in the cold,
Stories of the brave and bold.
An enchanted world unfolds,
In the lattice, dreams retold.

Snowflakes dance on frosted air,
In their beauty, magic rare.
Glimpses of the unseen light,
Filling hearts with pure delight.

As dusk descends, the stars appear,
Casting wishes, drawing near.
Winter's grace, a timeless art,
Magic dwells within the heart.

The Magic of Crystalline Dreams

In the still of night, stars gleam bright,
Whispers of magic in the silver light.
A dance of shadows, soft and rare,
Crystalline visions float in the air.

Through the forest deep, secrets hide,
In the heart of dreams where wonders abide.
Each spark a promise, a radiant scheme,
We drift through the magic of crystalline dream.

Moonbeams shimmer on a silken stream,
Reflecting the thoughts that flow like cream.
In every heartbeat, a story unfolds,
Wrapped in the warmth that the night holds.

With every breath, the world comes alive,
In the warmth of the magic, we thrive.
A tapestry woven with threads of gold,
In crystalline dreams, our souls are consoled.

So linger a while, let your heart soar,
In a world of wonder, forever explore.
For in these moments, so pure and bright,
The magic of dreams ignites the night.

Fleeting Illusions in the Chilled Air

In whispered winds, the stories wane,
Fleeting illusions, a subtle refrain.
Chilled air carries echoes of laughter,
As dreams weave patterns, chasing disaster.

Misty dawn spills whispers of fate,
The world awakens, yet gravely late.
Frost-kissed petals shiver on trees,
In this moment, the heart finds ease.

Castles in clouds begin to fade,
Illusions linger, but memories invade.
The chill wraps close like a lover's embrace,
A fleeting touch of a lost time's grace.

As daylight breaks, shadows retreat,
Footprints of dreams beneath our feet.
Fleeting moments, like snowflakes trace,
In the chilled air, we find our place.

Yet memories linger; ghosts entwined,
Through mist and smoke, they've been confined.
Illusions drift on a sighing breeze,
In the heart of winter, we hum with ease.

Reflections of Winter in a Faerie's Heart

In the quiet glen where the faeries play,
Winter's breath kisses the end of day.
Glistening snowflakes like tiny stars,
Reflecting the world from afar.

A faerie's heart beats soft and light,
Cradled in shadows, embraced by night.
With each flutter, dreams weave anew,
Reflections of winter in every hue.

Whispers of frost paint the branches white,
While moonlit visions dance in the light.
Through silvered woods, they twirl and spin,
In the heart of a faerie, joy begins.

Frosted laughter fills the air,
Magic in moments, delicate and rare.
As night descends, promises spark,
In winter's embrace, the dreams ignite.

Graced by the stillness, time bends low,
The faerie's heart knows the dance, the glow.
With winter's touch, we find our way,
In reflections of magic, let us sway.

The Gleaming Frost of Whimsy's Night

A night of whimsy under the moon,
Where shadows hum a soft, sweet tune.
Gleaming frost blankets the crooked path,
In this world where dreams often bath.

Stars wink down from their velvet beds,
While stories dance in the faerie's heads.
The chill brings laughter, bright and bold,
As fables weave through the night's cold hold.

With each step stepping on fragile ice,
Whimsy twinkles, a pattern so nice.
In the frigid air, magic ignites,
The gleaming frost of whimsical nights.

Hushed laughter spills from the hearts that know,
The secrets hidden where cold winds blow.
A tapestry of sparkles, silver and bright,
Guides enchanted souls through the smothering night.

As dawn approaches, the spell will fade,
But the heart remembers the dreams it made.
Forever keeping that magic in sight,
In the gleaming frost of whimsy's night.

Delicate Crystals on Enchanted Breezes

Whispers of frost dance through the air,
Crystals glimmer, weaving a rare snare.
Each breath a shimmer, pure and bright,
Transforming dreams into the night.

Gentle winds carry tales untold,
Of shimmering wonders, brave and bold.
Beneath the moon's watchful embrace,
Nature's art finds its perfect place.

In every flake, a story spun,
Of laughter, silence, and winter's fun.
As stars align in the frosty skies,
Delicate magic before our eyes.

Every moment, a fleeting chance,
To catch a glimpse, to join the dance.
With open hearts, we shall explore,
The delicate crystals forevermore.

The Secrets of Silvered Shadows

In twilight's grasp, shadows play,
Silver whispers, here to stay.
Hidden stories, soft and deep,
In every corner, secrets sleep.

Moonlit paths lead us astray,
Footprints lost in the cool decay.
In the silence, echoes blend,
Inviting hearts to comprehend.

A dance of light through branches bare,
Silver glimmers light as air.
Nature's canvas, brushed with care,
Whispers of magic linger there.

The night unveils its cloak of dreams,
Where nothing is quite as it seems.
Beneath the shadows, truths align,
In stillness, our souls intertwine.

Glacial Petals in the Garden of Frost

In gardens where the cold winds sigh,
Glacial petals twinkle, shy.
A frozen dance on winter's breath,
Life wrapped soft in a chill of death.

Beneath the ice, a secret bloom,
Echoes of spring in the frozen gloom.
Petals glinting in a radiant glow,
The heart of winter, a gentle show.

Every layer, a story kept,
Whispers of life where shadows crept.
In frozen beauty, dreams arise,
Glistening under the pale blue skies.

Upon the wind, a silent prayer,
For warmth to come, to break the snare.
In the garden where frost has kissed,
Silent wonders beckon, not to be missed.

Whimsy and Wonder at Winter's Door

As winter knocks, the world transforms,
Whimsy dances in chilly swarms.
Joyful laughter fills the air,
A tapestry of magic, rare.

Frosty breath upon our cheeks,
In the stillness, adventure speaks.
Together, we embrace the chill,
Hearts aglow with warmth and thrill.

Through snow-draped trees, shadows play,
Guiding us through the frosty gray.
With every step, a spark ignites,
Whimsy's charm in winter nights.

At winter's door, the world is bright,
Where dreams mingle with soft twilight.
In this moment, we will soar,
Bound by wonder, forevermore.

The Frosted Path of Dreams Forgotten

Silent whispers in the night,
Lost echoes in silver light.
Footsteps fade on frozen ground,
In shadows where hopes are bound.

A breath of wind, a chill so deep,
Secrets that the moon does keep.
Each star flickers like a tear,
Memories of yesteryear.

Frosted branches, brittle sighs,
Underneath the endless skies.
Wanderers tread this silent maze,
In a world wrapped in a haze.

Time drips down like melting ice,
Lost treasures, a fleeting price.
Through the mist, the figures roam,
Searching still for a lost home.

In this realm of frost and dream,
Reality unravels at the seam.
Yet hope glimmers like a flame,
In hearts that still remember names.

Glacial Vows in the Heart of Winter

In the quiet of falling snow,
Promises that the cold winds sow.
Frozen fingers touch the earth,
Binding souls to love's cold birth.

Beneath the stars, two hearts align,
Glacial vows like twisted twine.
Chilled breaths weave a tapestry,
Of warmth in stark simplicity.

Moonlight spills on icy streams,
Reflecting all their silent dreams.
Hands clenched tight against the chill,
As time and stillness blend at will.

Footprints carved in sudden snow,
Each step taken, love's sweet glow.
Though winter's grasp may seem unkind,
In ice, a heat they both can find.

In the heart of winter's breath,
Life blooms brightly, defying death.
With every flake that graces ground,
They rise together, love unbound.

Snowlit Reveries Beneath the Faerie Canopy

In a forest draped in white,
Twinkling lights dance with delight.
Faeries whisper in the air,
Dreams unfold without a care.

Snowflakes swirl like tiny stars,
Creating magic, near and far.
Beneath the boughs, soft and low,
Wonders spark in silent flow.

Glimmers bright on frozen streams,
A world alive with gentle dreams.
Each shadow dances with a grace,
In this enchanted, hidden space.

Winter's breath holds tales of old,
Stories waiting to be told.
In the hush, a secret song,
Inviting all to sing along.

As morning breaks, the faeries gleam,
In the light of dawn's first beam.
Their laughter twirls as snowflakes fall,
In reveries that bind us all.

Cascade of Crystals in the Mystic Grove

Through the grove where silence reigns,
Crystal droplets, nature's chains.
Sparkling threads of icy lace,
Weave a dream in this sacred space.

Boughs entwined in shimmering light,
Reflecting echoes of the night.
Each step whispers ancient lore,
In a tapestry to explore.

Glistening paths through frozen leaves,
Where the world in silence weaves.
A cascade falls, soft and bright,
Guiding souls into the night.

Here, the air is sweet and clear,
Carried songs all lend an ear.
Nature cradles every sound,
As magic swirls upon the ground.

The mystic grove breathes soft and low,
Holding secrets only few know.
In crystal cascades, hearts embrace,
Found at last in this sacred place.

The Icebound Serenade of Dreams

In the hush of night, stars align,
Whispers of winter, softly entwine.
Crystal flakes kiss the ground below,
As frozen melodies begin to flow.

Shadows dance in the pale moonlight,
Chill of the season, a shimmering sight.
Echoes of laughter in frosty air,
Building a world beyond compare.

Trees stand tall in their white embrace,
Guardian spirits in this sacred space.
Through the silence, a symphony hums,
Found in the stillness, where magic comes.

Dreams weave softly through the night sky,
Under the watchful, twinkling eyes.
Each breath a cloud, each sigh a song,
In this wild winter, we all belong.

Beneath the glow of the silver light,
Hearts are warmed by the frosty bite.
In every corner, dreams intertwine,
An icebound serenade, pure and divine.

Faerie Wishes in a Winter's Hand

In the heart of frost, faeries play,
Skimming the snowflakes, light as a ray.
Wishing upon a glimmering star,
Hopes take flight, no matter how far.

Winter whispers with a gentle breath,
Dreams take root in the chill of death.
Each sigh of the night, a tale untold,
Magic weaves stories from memories old.

Tiny footprints in shimmering white,
Leading us deeper into the night.
Echoes of laughter, soft and sweet,
Faerie wishes dance on frosty feet.

Through crystalline realms where shadows bend,
Secrets of winter begin to mend.
In every swirl of the cold, crisp air,
Lies a promise, a wish laid bare.

So close your eyes and take a leap,
Into the dreams that winter keeps.
In this hush, where wonders blend,
Faerie wishes, our hearts they send.

Glints of Light in the Frost's Embrace

Morning breaks with a silver gleam,
Frosty tendrils in the sunlight beam.
Glistening whispers on crisp, white grass,
Golden hues in the shadows pass.

Icicles hang like delicate chandeliers,
Reflecting stories from forgotten years.
Each glint of light paints the world anew,
A tapestry woven in frosts of blue.

The air is filled with a gentle chill,
Yet warmth is found in the quiet thrill.
Nature smiles in the sun's sweet rays,
Illuminating the cold, wintry ways.

Beneath the snow, life softly stirs,
Unseen magic, the heart concurs.
In this embrace, we find our place,
Softly held in the frost's embrace.

Through the silence, a promise glows,
A world reborn as the winter flows.
Glints of light in the frosty air,
Hold the secrets of seasons rare.

Whispered Secrets Beneath a Frosty Veil

Underneath the frost, secrets sleep,
Cradled softly in the night's deep steep.
Snowflakes spiral like whispers of air,
Each one a story, tender and rare.

In twilight shadows, dreams take form,
Beneath the surface, a quiet storm.
Voices echo in the still of night,
Luring us closer to the hidden light.

The world is hushed in a silvery glow,
Unraveling tales of the soft, white snow.
Each breath a secret, each moment pure,
In the heart of winter, we find our cure.

Frosty veils cloak the landscape bright,
Muffling sounds and holding them tight.
Within the quiet, a magic thrives,
Whispered secrets that the winter derives.

So linger here in this frozen dream,
Where the silence speaks and heartbeats teem.
Beneath the frost, we find our way,
In whispered secrets that softly sway.

Enchantment in Every Glittering Breath

In the twilight's soft embrace,
Magic dances in the air.
Every whisper, every trace,
Sugared dreams beyond compare.

Stars entwine with silver threads,
Woven into night's sweet song.
Each heartbeat gently spreads,
Harmony where souls belong.

Moonlight shimmers on the stream,
Reflecting hopes, a tender glow.
In this world, we dare to dream,
Together where the wildflowers grow.

Joyfully we chase the light,
Hand in hand through fields of gold.
With each step, the heart takes flight,
In this tale, love's saga told.

Let the stars guide us tonight,
Through enchantment's wondrous door.
In every breath, pure delight,
Forever we will seek for more.

Starlit Frost upon the Enchanted Path

Upon the path where shadows sway,
Starlit frost begins to twinkle.
Every step a dance, a play,
Nature's magic makes us crinkle.

The moonlight kisses the trees,
As whispers float on icy air.
Gentle echoes in the breeze,
Carrying dreams beyond compare.

Frosted leaves in silver shrouds,
A canvas of stories untold.
Gathering above the crowds,
Nature's wonders, rich as gold.

In this realm of sweet repose,
Time stands still, a sacred trust.
Underneath the starry clothes,
We find peace in cosmic dust.

Every glimmer, every hue,
Guiding us through darkened nights.
In this magic, pure and true,
We embrace our soul's delights.

Chilling Glimmer over Dreamland's Edge

A chilling glimmer lights the way,
Over dreamland's velvet crest.
As whispers of the night softly play,
Hopes and fears find peaceful rest.

Mirrored in a quiet lake,
Stars reflect their spectral light.
Every ripple that we make,
Guides us through the velvet night.

Magic weaves a soothing tale,
With every breath of frozen air.
In this world where dreams prevail,
We discover joys laid bare.

Around us sparkles, twinkling bright,
Magic cradled in the snow.
In the silence of the night,
Luminous paths begin to glow.

So let us wander, hand in hand,
Where mystery and dreams collide.
In this enchanting, frosted land,
Our hearts align, in love we bide.

Frosted Dreams on a Night's Whisper

On a night where whispers roam,
Frosted dreams take gentle flight.
In the stillness, find your home,
Wrapped in wonder, pure delight.

Snowflakes dance on breath of air,
Painting stories with their grace.
In this magic, hearts laid bare,
We discover time and space.

Echoes linger in the night,
Speaking secrets, soft and true.
Illuminated by starlight,
Together, me and you.

Every moment, fleeting yet,
In each heartbeat, memories twine.
Frosted dreams we won't forget,
In this realm where souls align.

So let us cherish, side by side,
Every whisper, every sigh.
In this dreamworld, love is our guide,
As the night begins to fly.

Chilled Petals in the Secrets of Night

In the dark where whispers dwell,
Petals sleep, their stories swell.
Moonlight drapes a silver coat,
Softly singing dreams afloat.

Gentle breezes sway and twine,
Secrets shared, a hidden sign.
In the stillness, hearts confess,
Chilled petals, sweet tenderness.

Stars above, like diamonds gleam,
Echoes of a midnight dream.
Crickets chant a lullaby,
While shadows dance, the night slips by.

Softly falls the dew's embrace,
Nature weaves a tranquil lace.
Underneath the velvet sky,
Chilled petals whisper, and sigh.

Night unfolds her cloak of peace,
In every breath, a chance to seize.
As dawn approaches, light ignites,
Chilled petals fade in morning's heights.

Ethereal Frost on Gossamer Wings

In twilight's grasp, a shimmer glows,
Ethereal frost on soft-winged throes.
Delicate strands of icy lace,
Dance through air, with gentle grace.

Whispers carried on winter's breath,
Life's fragile dream, a dance with death.
Gossamer wings, in silence soar,
Chasing shadows, forevermore.

Crystalline patterns on silent trees,
Nature's beauty, like a soft tease.
Each flake a story, unique and bright,
Ethereal visions in the night.

As dawn breaks soft, these wonders fade,
Leaving a world, enchanting, laid.
In memories spun, they still remain,
Ethereal frost, our hearts' refrain.

Let the chill embrace the heart,
A fleeting touch, never to part.
On gossamer wings, let dreams take flight,
Through the magic of the night.

Crystallized Echoes in the Silent Hollow

In the hollow where shadows speak,
Crystallized echoes, soft and meek.
Every sound a ghostly trace,
Reverberating time and space.

Underneath the star-strewn sky,
Memories linger, never die.
Whispers drift on winter air,
Crystallized dreams, scattered everywhere.

A timeless realm where seasons pause,
Nature's wonders without cause.
Echoes dance through the ancient trees,
Caressing hearts with gentle ease.

In silence deep, the world holds fast,
Moments captured, forever cast.
Crystallized echoes, we embrace,
In this hollow, a sacred space.

Reach within, let the stillness guide,
Through every tear and hidden tide.
In the silent hollow, we find peace,
Crystallized echoes, heartbeats cease.

Frost-Kissed Treasures of the Twilight Realm

In twilight's realm, where shadows weave,
Frost-kissed treasures subtly breathe.
Nature's bounty crowned in white,
Glistening softly in fading light.

Glistening petals, a dazzling sight,
Wrapped in frost, gleam pure and bright.
Every corner, a jewel concealed,
In twilight's grasp, beauty revealed.

Whispers of wonder in the air,
Frost-kissed secrets lay hidden there.
Collect the gems of silent grace,
In every moment, life's embrace.

As shadows stretch and night descends,
Frosted dreams become our friends.
Unlock the beauty, let it flow,
In twilight's realm, our spirits grow.

With every breath, the magic lingers,
Frost-kissed treasures on our fingers.
In the hush of dusk's sweet song,
Twilight's realm, where we belong.

Frost-Draped Dusk in a Hidden Realm

Whispers of night on the chilly breeze,
Silver stars peek through the frosted trees.
Moonlight dances on the frozen ground,
In this hidden realm, magic is found.

Crystals glisten like diamonds rare,
Soft shadows play in the evening air.
The world grows still, a tranquil embrace,
Time drifts away in this secret place.

A blanket of frost, serene and bright,
Envelops the land in shimmering light.
Dreams intertwine with the dusk's soft sighs,
In the heart of the realm where silence lies.

Gentle echoes of a faerie tune,
Stir the stillness under the moon.
Frost-draped branches weave tales untold,
In the grasp of night, their magic unfolds.

The stars bear witness to wonders unspun,
As warmth of the hearth threatens the fun.
Yet here in the dusk, all worries cease,
In this hidden realm, there's only peace.

Glacial Echoes of the Faerie Song

In a realm where the ice gently sings,
Glacial echoes from nature's wings.
Faerie voices rise, soft and clear,
Stirring the silence, enchanting the ear.

Each note carried by the whispering wind,
Crafts an allure that will never rescind.
Crystalline laughter under sunrise glow,
Inviting the heart where the wonder flows.

Frosted landscapes, aglow with delight,
Breathe life into dreams that take flight.
Ephemeral moments twirl through the air,
In glacial echoes, there's magic to share.

With every note, a story is spun,
Of ancient magic and shadows that run.
Where glistening snowflakes compose the score,
In a symphony of whispers, forevermore.

Underneath the vast velvet skies,
The chorus of nature never dies.
Held in the stillness, a song so sweet,
Glacial echoes make the heart beat.

Pearls of Frost on the Wandering Wind

Wandering winds carry tales of the night,
Whispered secrets, soft and light.
Pearls of frost shimmer, a delicate lace,
Adorning the world in a crystalline grace.

With each breath of chill, stories unfold,
Of adventures hidden and treasures untold.
Glimmers of beauty in every soft sigh,
Finding their way as the dreams drift by.

Upon the branches, a glistening sheen,
Reflecting the magic of what might have been.
Under the gaze of the moon's gentle glow,
Whispers of faeries in the frost-covered snow.

The dance of the wind brings a flicker of light,
Chasing shadows that linger in flight.
Pearls of frost sparkle like stars in a dream,
Riding the currents, a glimmering stream.

Yet in the stillness, the heartbeats align,
As the wandering wind weaves hope through the pine.
Nature's own treasure, so fragile and grand,
Pearls of frost, in a magical land.

A Chromatic Chill in Faerie Tides

Tides of faerie swirl in chromatic hues,
A chill dances softly, awakening the clues.
Glowing reflections on the water's face,
Where dreams and reality intertwine in grace.

Each wave a whisper, a secret untold,
Drawing us closer with stories of old.
Fleeting visions where colors collide,
In the embrace of the luminous tide.

Ocean's breath carries a crystalline sound,
In the currents of magic, where wonders abound.
A symphony of light in every caress,
The chill of the air makes the heart feel blessed.

As twilight descends, the colors ignite,
Painting the shore with bold, brilliant light.
Faerie tides beckon our spirits to rise,
In a world alive under starlit skies.

Caught in the moment, the magic held tight,
Igniting the dreams in the hush of the night.
A chromatic chill that sets spirits free,
Bound to the essence of what's meant to be.

Ethereal Frost-Kissed Reveries

In twilight's embrace, whispers unfold,
A dance of frost on dreams that are bold.
Silvery trails where starlight weaves,
In silent echoes, the heart believes.

Moonlit pathways, a shimmering glide,
Memories twinkle, in shadows they hide.
Every breath caught in winter's soft grasp,
Ethereal visions, in stillness we clasp.

Glistening fragments of whispers untold,
Each glimmering moment a story of old.
Through crystal realms, wandering we roam,
In frost-kissed reveries, we find our home.

Veils of white cloak the world anew,
A tapestry woven with silvery dew.
With every heartbeat, enchantment unfolds,
Eternity dances in wonders it holds.

Dreams flicker lightly like lanterns aglow,
Guiding the way where the chill winds blow.
In ethereal realms, we savor the night,
Frost-kissed and free, bathed in soft light.

Glistening Shadows Beneath the Twilight Veil

Under twilight's gaze, secrets are spun,
Glistening shadows where day's gone undone.
Whispers of dusk call from deep within,
Entwined in twilight, our journey begins.

Silken dreams float on a breeze so light,
Fleeting moments blend dark with the bright.
Stars peek out from their velvet retreat,
In this twilight realm, our hearts softly beat.

Echoes of laughter in the twilight's haze,
Guiding our footsteps through twilight's maze.
Where each flicker and shadow reside,
In the stillness, our secrets confide.

Draped in beauty, the world holds its breath,
A canvas alive, where shadows meet depth.
Glimmers of hope paint the sky with grace,
We find our place in the night's warm embrace.

Beneath the veil where these dreams intertwine,
Every heartbeat feels like a whisper divine.
With glistening shadows that dance on the waves,
Twilight cradles us, our spirits it saves.

Frozen Echoes from a Mystical Past

In the hush of twilight, echoes remain,
Frozen whispers of joy and of pain.
Footsteps of time on the snow softly tread,
Where memories linger, where dreams are not dead.

Like frost on the window, the past softly glows,
Tales of enchantment in silence that flows.
Through the crystal night, histories sing,
Frozen echoes of what memories bring.

Specters of laughter, of love long since lost,
Each shimmering moment reveals what it cost.
In every flake's fall, a story is spun,
A tapestry woven where time comes undone.

Whirling in air are the visions of yore,
Guiding us gently to doors left before.
An echo of whispers, a haunting refrain,
In the depths of the silence, our hearts feel the strain.

With every soft breeze, the past calls to us,
Through frozen echoes, we long to discuss,
The beauty of moments that shaped our heart's tune,
In the mystic embrace of a silver-cast moon.

Glacial Threads of Enchantment

In the realm of frost, where wonders entwine,
Glacial threads weave a tapestry divine.
Draped in white whispers, the world starts to glow,
As dreams drift like snowflakes, suspended in flow.

Enchantment flows gently through branches and leaves,
Carried on breezes, the cold soul believes.
Each crystalline flake sings a soft lullaby,
Against the backdrop of an infinite sky.

Within frozen depths, the magic resides,
Guiding lost hearts where true love abides.
Every moment a sparkle, each breath a delight,
In glacial enchantment, we dance through the night.

Echoes of laughter through frosty terrains,
In the heart of the ice, where joy still remains.
Wrapped in the silence of winter's embrace,
Glacial threads beckon, inviting our grace.

As shadows stretch long and twilight descends,
In this magical place, our journey transcends.
We follow the whispers, the stories they weave,
In glacial enchantment, we learn to believe.

Beneath the Frosty Boughs of Mystical Woods

Beneath the frost, the boughs do sway,
Whispers of night in silvery gray.
Shadows dance in a spectral glow,
Secrets of winter the cold winds blow.

Footsteps light on the delicate frost,
Nature's embrace, no beauty lost.
Echoes of magic in every breath,
Life intertwined with whispers of death.

Twinkling stars through branches peek,
Moonlit paths where silence speaks.
The air is crisp, a calm so deep,
In dreams of the woods, the heart shall leap.

Gentle sighs of the sleeping trees,
Time stands still with each soft breeze.
A world untouched, so pure, so wide,
Where nature's secrets and dreams abide.

Shards of Magic in the Crystal Glades

In crystal glades where light refracts,
Shards of magic in the air act.
Each breath a spell, each sigh a dream,
Whispers float on the moonlit stream.

Glimmers catch in the eyes of night,
Flickering realms of pure delight.
Dancing beams of ethereal hues,
Crafting tales that the night renews.

A path unfolds through the frozen mist,
Where every shadow holds a twist.
Nature's canvas, painted bright,
With every shard of magic's light.

Ethereal beings weave through the trees,
Soft laughter carried by the breeze.
In the stillness, a song takes flight,
Echoes of wonder in the heart of night.

Enchanted Sprigs Under a Frozen Sky

Enchanted sprigs under frozen sky,
Whispers of magic that flutter by.
Frosted leaves in a silvery dream,
Nature's wonders in a gentle gleam.

Stars twinkle in their ethereal dance,
Every moment holds a fleeting chance.
In the stillness, enchantment grows,
Under the sky where the pure wind blows.

The nightingale sings a lullaby sweet,
Through icy branches, her song is fleet.
Yet beneath the frost lies vibrant life,
Waiting for spring, beyond the strife.

With every breath, the air does sing,
A promise held on winter's wing.
In shadows cast by the moon's soft light,
Hope finds a way to break through the night.

Silvery Gleams in the Whispering Snow

Silvery gleams in the whispering snow,
Softly it blankets the world below.
Each flake a whisper, a tale to tell,
Of dreams embraced in a frosty spell.

Footprints vanish in the delicate white,
Muffled sounds of a tranquil night.
The world transformed, a glistening sheet,
Where every heartbeat finds its beat.

Beneath the veil, old magic stirs,
Echoing softly as the winter blurs.
In the stillness, the heart finds peace,
In the simple moments, fears release.

Twinkling lights on the branches sway,
Guiding lost souls along the way.
Nature's breath in the twilight's gleam,
A world enchanted, wrapped in a dream.

The Mystique of the Frozen Faerie Path

In twilight's grasp, the faerie's glow,
A silent path where whispers flow.
Snowflakes dance on gentle breeze,
Secrets held among the trees.

Silvery frost adorns the ground,
In every step, magic is found.
Footprints lead, yet none remain,
Only shadows of delight and pain.

Crystals twinkle, a fleeting spark,
Where dreams are whispered in the dark.
Underneath the starlit sky,
The faerie path winds, oh so sly.

Soft laughter lingers, sweet and bright,
Guiding travelers through the night.
Each turn brings a tale anew,
In this world of wonder, so true.

The frozen realm, a beauty rare,
Calls to the heart with gentle care.
Along this trail, the stories weave,
As night falls, and we believe.

Beneath the Glittering Canopy of Dreams

In a forest draped in silver light,
Stars hang low, a breathtaking sight.
Dreams take flight on whispers of air,
As moonlit beams weave through the hair.

Beneath the boughs, where shadows play,
Time stands still, night turns to day.
A carpet of petals, soft and rare,
Each one glimmers, magic laid bare.

The canopy glistens, a celestial dome,
Calling the wanderers far from home.
Each star a wish, crafted in glow,
Beneath its embrace, our spirits grow.

Voices echo from trees so grand,
Stretched like fingers of a guiding hand.
In the depths of night, serenity gleams,
All is possible beneath our dreams.

As dawn approaches, the magic fades,
Yet memories linger in sunlit glades.
A promise whispers, forever it seems,
Beneath the glittering canopy of dreams.

Enchanted Frost on a Moonlit Journey

In stillness reigns the winter's breath,
A journey carved, between life and death.
The moon's soft glow, a gentle guide,
On frosted paths, where secrets hide.

Each step a story, etched in ice,
Whispers of faeries, soft and precise.
The chill wraps close, a tender embrace,
Tracing the lines of time and space.

Through silver oaks, shadows leap,
Into the night, dreams softly creep.
A tapestry woven in glimmering frost,
With every heartbeat, we cherish the lost.

In echoes of laughter, the night lights dance,
Inviting the brave to take a chance.
Stars twirl above like notes of a song,
Echoing rhythms where we belong.

Enchanted frost, a beautiful sight,
Guiding our souls in the depths of night.
With every breath, we're drawn even near,
On this moonlit journey, we conquer our fear.

Dazzling Chill of the Faerie Whisper

In the heart of night, a chill descends,
Where time suspends and magic blends.
A faerie whisper, soft and low,
Guides us forward where dreams may flow.

Dazzling hues in the realms of dark,
Each glimmering shimmer ignites a spark.
Frosted petals beneath our feet,
Every heartbeat's rhythm, a lilting beat.

A hidden glade, where secrets breathe,
In silken webs, the past we weave.
The air electrified, charged with delight,
As magic swirls in the velvet night.

Spirits dance in the shimmering light,
Inviting us in with hearts so bright.
We reach for joy, and it beckons clear,
In the dazzling chill, we cast off our fear.

As dawn awakes and shadows recede,
The faerie whisper plants a seed.
A fleeting touch, forever remains,
In the soul's deep echo, love entertains.

Whispering Frost on Ancient Stones

On ancient stones, the frost confides,
The secrets of the time it hides.
Whispers soft like a gentle sigh,
Underneath the winter sky.

Moonlight dances on the cold,
As stories of the past unfold.
Each crack and crevice, a tale retold,
In frost-kissed silence, brave and bold.

Nature's canvas, white and bright,
A tapestry of pure delight.
Echoes linger, faint and clear,
A frozen voice for those who hear.

Among the ages, shadows play,
With every dawn and dusk's decay.
The frost caresses, soft and slow,
Ancient stones, a lovely glow.

Through the night, the chill expands,
Its delicate touch on rugged lands.
Creating wonders, lost in time,
Whispering frost, a silent rhyme.

The Frost Weaves Tales of Enchantment

In every breath, the frost weaves tales,
Of hidden realms and ethereal trails.
Softly it covers the world in white,
Crafting magic in the still of night.

Frozen petals gleam like stars,
Whispers of beauty carried from afar.
Glistening threads in the morning light,
A tapestry spun with pure delight.

Creeping tendrils, a chilly embrace,
Adorning every hidden place.
With every breeze, it starts to sing,
Bringing warmth to the chill of spring.

A dance of shimmers across the ground,
In nature's cradle, stories abound.
The frost, a keeper of dreams untold,
In its grip, enchantment unfolds.

With every dawn, the magic fades,
Yet in our hearts, the beauty invades.
Frost weaves softly, a gentle call,
Tales of enchantment, cherished by all.

Crystal Dawn in the Faerie Glade

Dewdrops sparkle like diamonds bright,
Beneath the glow of morning light.
In the faerie glade where shadows dance,
Magic unfolds in a sparkling trance.

Whispers echo through the trees,
Carried lightly by the breeze.
Glistening leaves, a mystical show,
As the dawn ignites the world below.

Crystal petals, soft and rare,
Adorn each branch with tender care.
In the embrace of nature's grace,
Faeries gather in their hidden space.

Every moment here is still,
Suspended time, a gentle thrill.
As sunlight breaks, it softly glows,
In faerie glades, enchantment flows.

Awake, the dreams of night take flight,
In crystal dawn, the world feels right.
Whispers linger, magic imbued,
In every corner, nature's mood.

Shimmering Shadows in the Chilled Night

Underneath the starry veil,
Shadows whisper a timeless tale.
The night is crisp, the air so still,
In shimmering darkness, hearts can fill.

Cold winds carry a haunting song,
As silent echoes of night belong.
Stars above twinkle with delight,
Guiding lost souls through the night.

Each step echoes on frozen ground,
In the chill, soft whispers surround.
Shadows flicker, teasing the eye,
As dreams entwine and spirits fly.

Moonbeams weave through branches bare,
Illuminating secrets we dare.
In the quiet, wisdom flows,
In shimmering shadows, mystery grows.

From dusk till dawn, the night prevails,
With stories etched in soft night trails.
Chilled whispers wrap the world tight,
In shimmering shadows, we find light.

Drifting Snowflakes of Forgotten Tales

Drifting snowflakes softly weave,
Each flake a tale we can't perceive.
Whispers of moments long gone by,
In the chill of winter's sigh.

They touch the ground, a silent grace,
Hiding memories in their embrace.
Fragile stories, caught in time,
In a world of peace, so sublime.

Winds carry them, a fleeting dream,
In the twilight glow, they softly gleam.
Nature's art, on canvas white,
Painting whispers in the night.

Each snowflake a wish, pure and bright,
Clinging close till the morning light.
They melt away but not in vain,
For tales remain in cold's refrain.

From frosty realms to hearts so warm,
Each drifting flake a soothing charm.
In their descent, a dance so free,
Guarding secrets of memory.

A Dance of Crystals in the Enchanted Forest

Crystals dance in moonlit glee,
In an enchanted forest, wild and free.
Glowing softly through the trees,
A symphony whispered by the breeze.

Each twirl reveals a hidden light,
Sparkling bright in the still of night.
Leaves glisten with a silver hue,
Nature's magic softly shines through.

Fairy laughter fills the air,
A waltz of wonders everywhere.
In this realm, time stands still,
Embraced by dreams and nature's thrill.

Under starlit skies, they play,
Guided by the night's ballet.
With every shimmer, hearts entwine,
In a dance that's truly divine.

Crystalline echoes of love's embrace,
In the forest's heart, find your place.
For when the night draws near, you'll see,
The dance of crystals sets us free.

The Whisper of Winter in the Faerie's Realm

In the faerie realm, winter sings,
Whispers of snow on delicate wings.
Frosty breath of the night unfolds,
Cradling warmth in its icy holds.

Moonbeams flicker on leaves of jade,
A shimmering veil that never fades.
Crystal laughter spills through the night,
Nature awakens, pure delight.

Amidst the trees, shadows play,
As winter weaves its soft ballet.
Echoes of magic, silent and bright,
Invite the dreamers to join the flight.

Glistening paths where children roam,
Each frosted step feels like home.
In the hush of the winter's gaze,
The faerie's whispers set ablaze.

Under the stars, dreams take flight,
In the embrace of the frosty night.
With every breath, a story to tell,
In the whispers of winter's spell.

Frosty Glimmers in a Twilight Spell

In twilight's glow, frost begins to gleam,
A tapestry woven from a chill's dream.
Softly glowing in shades of blue,
A whispering breath of the coming dew.

Glimmers dance on the edges of night,
Painting the world in silvery light.
Each frosty breath holds secrets to share,
In the embrace of the cool night air.

The stars awaken with a twinkle bright,
Guiding the lost through the velvet night.
Paths of ice where shadows blend,
In the stillness, all worries suspend.

A canvas of frost, nature's soft art,
Inviting us to play our part.
With frosty glimmers, dreams will swell,
In the magic of twilight's spell.

So bow to the night, release your soul,
Let glimmers of frost make you whole.
In every twinkle, a world to explore,
In twilight's arms, we dream forevermore.